The COMPLETE Plan Book

The Complete Plan Book provides organization at your fingertips. Planning the school year becomes a cinch with a plan book that includes:

- Student information organizer pages
- Helpful monthly calendars with ample space for long-range planning
- 45 weeks of planning pages with plenty of space for recording lesson plans and a useful teacher tip for each week
- Essential classroom management reproducibles, such as a class roster, parent-teacher conference reports, and a programmable weekly newsletter

Name

Grade/Subject

School Name

School Address

School Phone Number

School E-Mail Address

School Year

Table of Contents:

Sample Planning Page	inside front cover
Student Information	2-3
Birthdays	4
Transportation Information	5
Planning Calendars	6-11
Substitute Information	12
Class Roster Reproducible	13
Classroom Management/Modifications	14-19
Parent-Teacher Conference Report Reproducible	20
Weekly Newsletter Reproducible	21
Weekly Planning Pages	22-111
Curriculum Web Sites	112

Student Information

#	Student Name	Birthday	Parent(s)/Guardian(s)	Address
1				
2				
3				
4				
5				
6				
7				
8				
9				
10				
11				
12				
13				
14				
15				
16				
17				
18				
19				
20				
21				
22				
23				
24				
25				
26				
27				
28				
29				
30				
31				
32				

Student Information

Home Phone	Work Phone	E-Mail Address	Transportation	Notes

Birthdays

August

September

October

November

December

January

February

March

April

May

June

July

Transportation Information

	Student Name	To School	From School
1			
2			
3			
4			
5			
6			
7			
8			
9			
10			
11			
12			
13			
14			
15			
16			
17			
18			
19			
20			
21			
22			
23			
24			
25			
26			
27			
28			
29			
30			
31			
32			

The COMPLETE Plan Book

Month of: _____

Monday	Tuesday	Wednesday	Thursday	Friday
○	○	○	○	○
○	○	○	○	○
○	○	○	○	○
○	○	○	○	○
○	○	○	○	○

Month of: _____

Monday	Tuesday	Wednesday	Thursday	Friday
○	○	○	○	○
○	○	○	○	○
○	○	○	○	○
○	○	○	○	○
○	○	○	○	○

© Carson-Dellosa • CD-104069

Month of: _____

Monday	Tuesday	Wednesday	Thursday	Friday
○	○	○	○	○
○	○	○	○	○
○	○	○	○	○
○	○	○	○	○
○	○	○	○	○

Month of: _____

The COMPLETE Plan Book

Monday	Tuesday	Wednesday	Thursday	Friday
○	○	○	○	○
○	○	○	○	○
○	○	○	○	○
○	○	○	○	○
○	○	○	○	○

The COMPLETE Plan Book

Month of: _____

Month of: _____

Monday	Tuesday	Wednesday	Thursday	Friday	Monday	Tuesday	Wednesday	Thursday	Friday
○	○	○	○	○	○	○	○	○	○
○	○	○	○	○	○	○	○	○	○
○	○	○	○	○	○	○	○	○	○
○	○	○	○	○	○	○	○	○	○
○	○	○	○	○	○	○	○	○	○

9 | Month of: _____

Month of: _____

The COMPLETE Plan Book

Monday	Tuesday	Wednesday	Thursday	Friday	Monday	Tuesday	Wednesday	Thursday	Friday
○	○	○	○	○	○	○	○	○	○
○	○	○	○	○	○	○	○	○	○
○	○	○	○	○	○	○	○	○	○
○	○	○	○	○	○	○	○	○	○
○	○	○	○	○	○	○	○	○	○

© Carson-Dellosa • CD-104069

The Complete Plan Book

Month of: _____

Month of: _____

Monday	Tuesday	Wednesday	Thursday	Friday	Monday	Tuesday	Wednesday	Thursday	Friday
○	○	○	○	○	○	○	○	○	○
○	○	○	○	○	○	○	○	○	○
○	○	○	○	○	○	○	○	○	○
○	○	○	○	○	○	○	○	○	○
○	○	○	○	○	○	○	○	○	○

Month of: _____					Month of: _____				
Monday	Tuesday	Wednesday	Thursday	Friday	Monday	Tuesday	Wednesday	Thursday	Friday
○	○	○	○	○	○	○	○	○	○
○	○	○	○	○	○	○	○	○	○
○	○	○	○	○	○	○	○	○	○
○	○	○	○	○	○	○	○	○	○
○	○	○	○	○	○	○	○	○	○

The COMPLETE Plan Book

Substitute Information

School Schedule
School Begins: _____
Lunch: _____
Recess: _____
Dismissal: _____
Other: _____

Important People
Grade Level Teachers: _____
Aide(s): _____
Reliable Students: _____
Principal: _____
Assistant Principal: _____
Secretary: _____
Nurse: _____
Guidance Counselor: _____
Parent Volunteers: _____

Classroom Procedures
Beginning Class: _____
Classroom Management/Discipline: _____
Lunch: _____
Recess: _____
Free Time: _____
Safety Drills: _____
Ending Class: _____
Other: _____

Special Classes
(Teacher Name, Day of Week, Time)
Music: _____
Art: _____
Physical Education: _____
Media: _____
Resource: _____
Other: _____

Special Needs
Name	Need
_____	_____
_____	_____

Other: _____

Class Roster

The COMPLETE Plan Book

NOTES

Classroom Management/Modifications

Student Name	Parent(s)/Guardian(s)	Date	Behavior	Action Taken	Result/Comments

Classroom Management/Modifications

Student Name	Parent(s)/Guardian(s)	Date	Behavior	Action Taken	Result/Comments

Classroom Management/Modifications

Student Name	Parent(s)/Guardian(s)	Date	Behavior	Action Taken	Result/Comments

Classroom Management/Modifications

Student Name	Parent(s)/Guardian(s)	Date	Behavior	Action Taken	Result/Comments

Classroom Management/Modifications

Student Name	Parent(s)/Guardian(s)	Date	Behavior	Action Taken	Result/Comments

Classroom Management/Modifications

Student Name	Parent(s)/Guardian(s)	Date	Behavior	Action Taken	Result/Comments

Parent-Teacher Conference Report

Date:
Student:
Attendees:

ACADEMIC PERFORMANCE

Strengths:

Areas That Need Improvement:

Teacher Comments:

Parent Comments:

Listening Skills:
Following Directions:
Effort/Motivation:
Participation:
Organizational Skills:
Assignments/Quality of Work
In-School:
Homework:
Assessments
Informal:
Formal:
Time Management:
Study Habits:

BEHAVIOR

Gets Along Well with Others:
Cooperative:
Shows Respect for Self and Others:
Responsible for Actions:

Student Signature (if applicable):
Parent Signature:
Teacher Signature:

NOTES

Weekly Newsletter

Weekly Newsletter

From the desk of: _____

Date: _____

Monday

Tuesday

Wednesday

Thursday

Friday

Special Activities/Events:

Other:

Week of _____	Subject Time					
Monday Date: Absences:	Take Note					
Tuesday Date: Absences:	Take Note					
Wednesday Date: Absences:	Take Note					
Thursday Date: Absences:	Take Note					
Friday Date: Absences:	Take Note					

Lesson Plan Page Tip

Cut off the upper right corners of lesson planning pages when you have completed the week in which those lessons were taught. That way, it will be a cinch to find the next week of planning pages. Just flip to the page that is visible (corner not cut off). It will make it easy for you to see that you have accomplished your weekly goals.

Things to Remember

Week of _____	Subject _____ Time					
Monday Date: Absences:	Take Note					
Tuesday Date: Absences:	Take Note					
Wednesday Date: Absences:	Take Note					
Thursday Date: Absences:	Take Note					
Friday Date: Absences:	Take Note					

© Carson-Dellosa • CD-104069

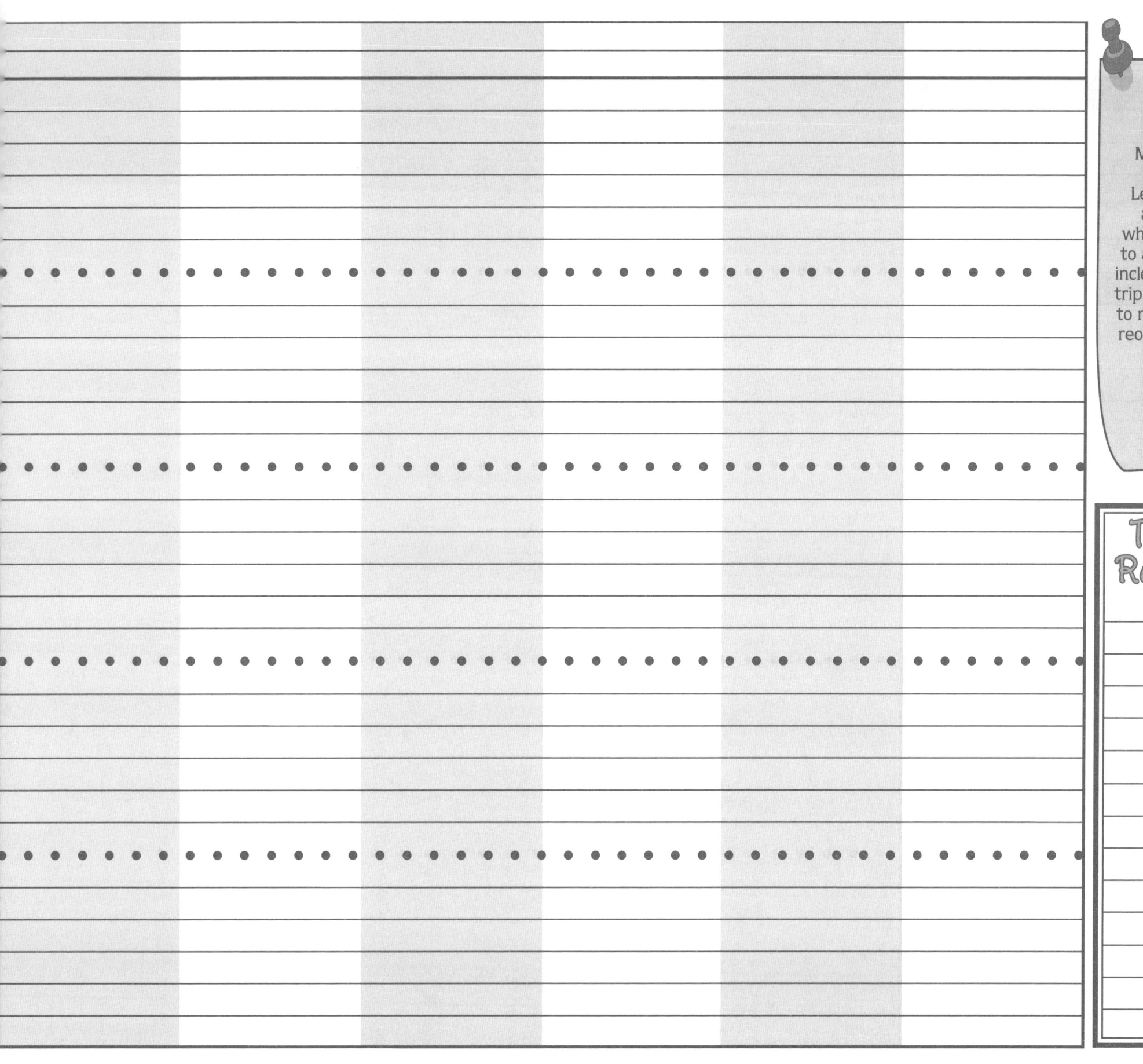

Planning in Pencil

Make sure to write your lesson plans in pencil. Lesson plans can change at a moment's notice, whether the change is due to an unexpected absence, inclement weather, or a field trip. Sometimes it is difficult to mark through, rewrite, or reorganize lesson plans that are written in ink.

Things to Remember

© Carson-Dellosa • CD-104069

Week of _____	Subject Time					
Monday Date: Absences:	Take Note					
Tuesday Date: Absences:	Take Note					
Wednesday Date: Absences:	Take Note					
Thursday Date: Absences:	Take Note					
Friday Date: Absences:	Take Note					

© Carson-Dellosa • CD-104069

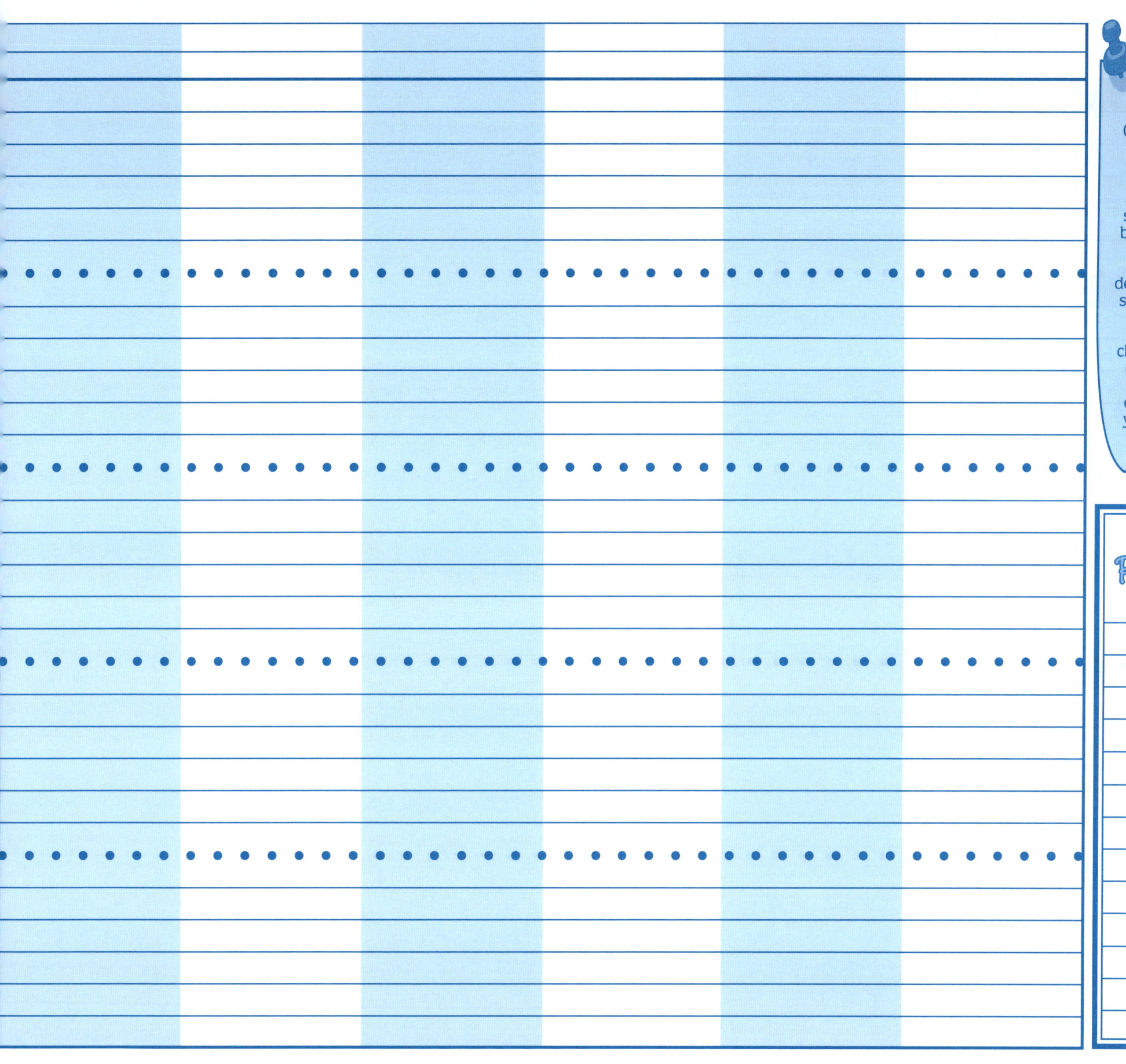

Organization: A Time-Saver

Organization in the classroom can equal less searching for lesson plan materials, more sticking to routines in your absence, and more student responsibility! At the beginning of each school year, recycle old files, duplicated reproducibles, damaged decorative materials, etc. Then, schedule time to organize and label files, materials, books, manipulatives, and other classroom necessities. If you fit organizational time into your schedule at the beginning of each school year, you increase your chances of accomplishing significant goals and tasks.

Things to Remember

Week of _____	Subject Time						
Monday Date: Absences:	Take Note						
Tuesday Date: Absences:	Take Note						
Wednesday Date: Absences:	Take Note						
Thursday Date: Absences:	Take Note						
Friday Date: Absences:	Take Note						

© Carson-Dellosa • CD-104069

All About Us

An "All About Me" activity at the beginning of the school year can be very helpful in creating a team-oriented atmosphere. Have students get more acquainted with each other by bringing in "Me" bags to share with their classmates. A "Me" bag is a small paper bag containing three or four items that represent a student (things she collects, family pictures, favorite book, etc.). Students will enjoy sharing and learning more about each other.

Things to Remember

Week of _____	Subject _____ Time					
Monday Date: Absences:	Take Note					
Tuesday Date: Absences:	Take Note					
Wednesday Date: Absences:	Take Note					
Thursday Date: Absences:	Take Note					
Friday Date: Absences:	Take Note					

Picture Our Growth

Help students learn about measurement with a fun, creative activity. At the beginning of the school year, take photos of students. Then, have them record their heights and other measurable characteristics (shoe sizes, head circumferences, etc.) on the backs of the photos. At the end of the school year, repeat the activity and have students compare their findings. Students will be amazed by the changes that occur over the school year.

Things to Remember

Week of _____	Subject Time					
Monday Date: Absences:	Take Note					
Tuesday Date: Absences:	Take Note					
Wednesday Date: Absences:	Take Note					
Thursday Date: Absences:	Take Note					
Friday Date: Absences:	Take Note					

© Carson-Dellosa • CD-104069

Emergency Information at Your Fingertips

Keep a copy of the class roster and emergency contact information in an envelope by the classroom door. You will avoid losing time searching for important information during safety drills or actual emergency events.

Things to Remember

Week of _____	Subject Time					
Monday Date: Absences:	Take Note					
Tuesday Date: Absences:	Take Note					
Wednesday Date: Absences:	Take Note					
Thursday Date: Absences:	Take Note					
Friday Date: Absences:	Take Note					

What's Happening?

Create a "What's Happening?" bulletin board display that will be versatile and useful throughout the entire school year. Use the display to post upcoming field trips, students' intramural sports activities, holidays, teacher workdays, due dates for academic projects, birthdays, assemblies, and more. Students and classroom visitors will find this visual reference informative and helpful.

Things to Remember

Week of _____	Subject Time					
Monday Date: Absences:	Take Note					
Tuesday Date: Absences:	Take Note					
Wednesday Date: Absences:	Take Note					
Thursday Date: Absences:	Take Note					
Friday Date: Absences:	Take Note					

Room Parent

Having a Room Parent can be helpful. As a valuable classroom volunteer, a Room Mom or Dad oversees important tasks such as planning class parties and calling parents for extra class supplies. Have parents sign up for this distinguished role at the beginning of the school year. Then, draw from the volunteers to find the right mom or dad for this rewarding volunteer job.

Things to Remember

Week of _____	Subject Time					
Monday Date: Absences:	Take Note					
Tuesday Date: Absences:	Take Note					
Wednesday Date: Absences:	Take Note					
Thursday Date: Absences:	Take Note					
Friday Date: Absences:	Take Note					

Homework Helpers

Create helpful homework folders using two-pocket portfolios. Designate one side of a folder for parent notes and/or information (for example, student work to be reviewed, field trip information, etc.). Designate the other side of the folder for student assignments. Both students and parents will know exactly where to look for items they need to complete, sign, or review.

Things to Remember

Week of _____	Subject Time					
Monday Date: Absences:	Take Note					
Tuesday Date: Absences:	Take Note					
Wednesday Date: Absences:	Take Note					
Thursday Date: Absences:	Take Note					
Friday Date: Absences:	Take Note					

© Carson-Dellosa • CD-104069

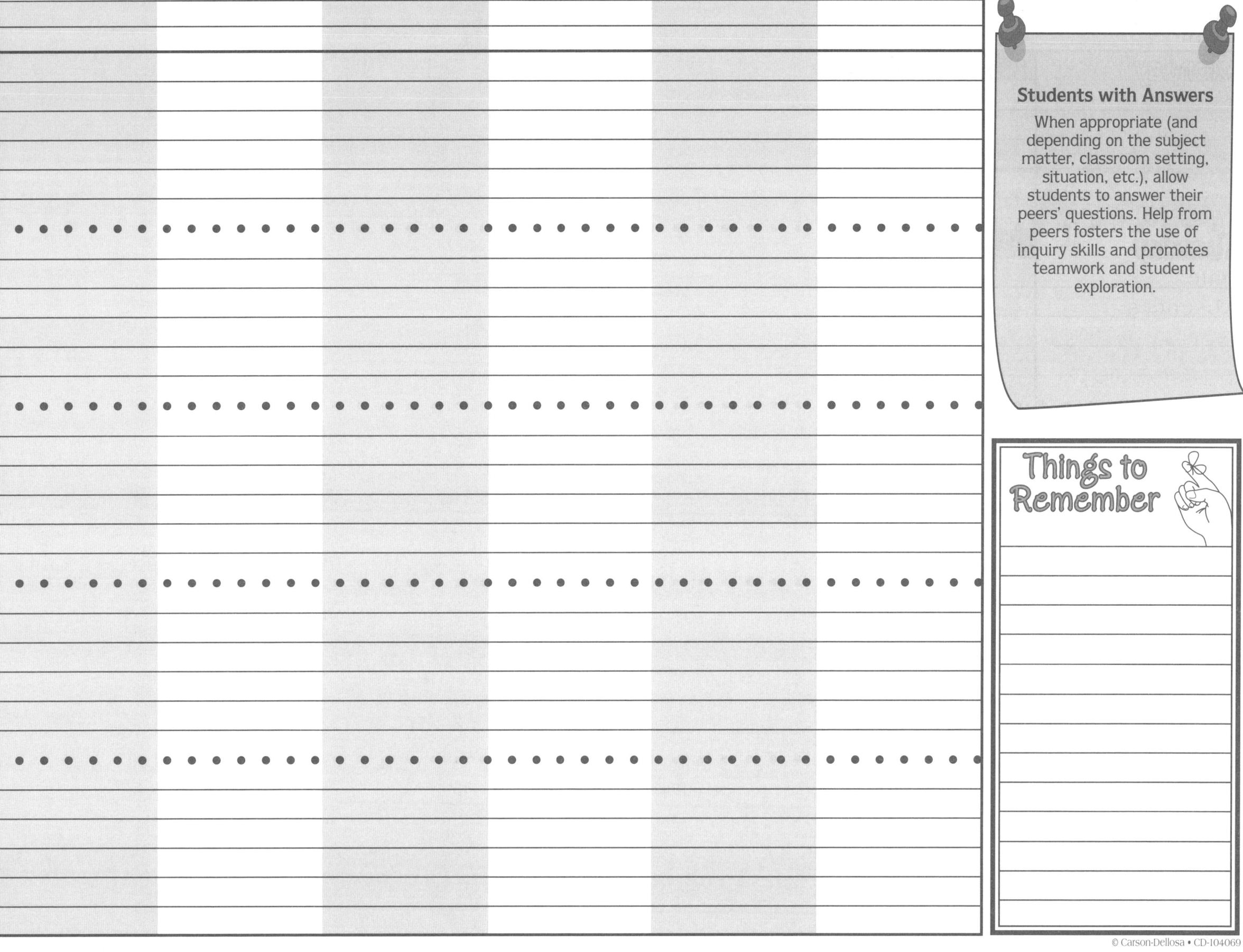

Students with Answers

When appropriate (and depending on the subject matter, classroom setting, situation, etc.), allow students to answer their peers' questions. Help from peers fosters the use of inquiry skills and promotes teamwork and student exploration.

Things to Remember

Week of_____	Subject _____ Time					
Monday Date: Absences:	Take Note					
Tuesday Date: Absences:	Take Note					
Wednesday Date: Absences:	Take Note					
Thursday Date: Absences:	Take Note					
Friday Date: Absences:	Take Note					

© Carson-Dellosa • CD-104069

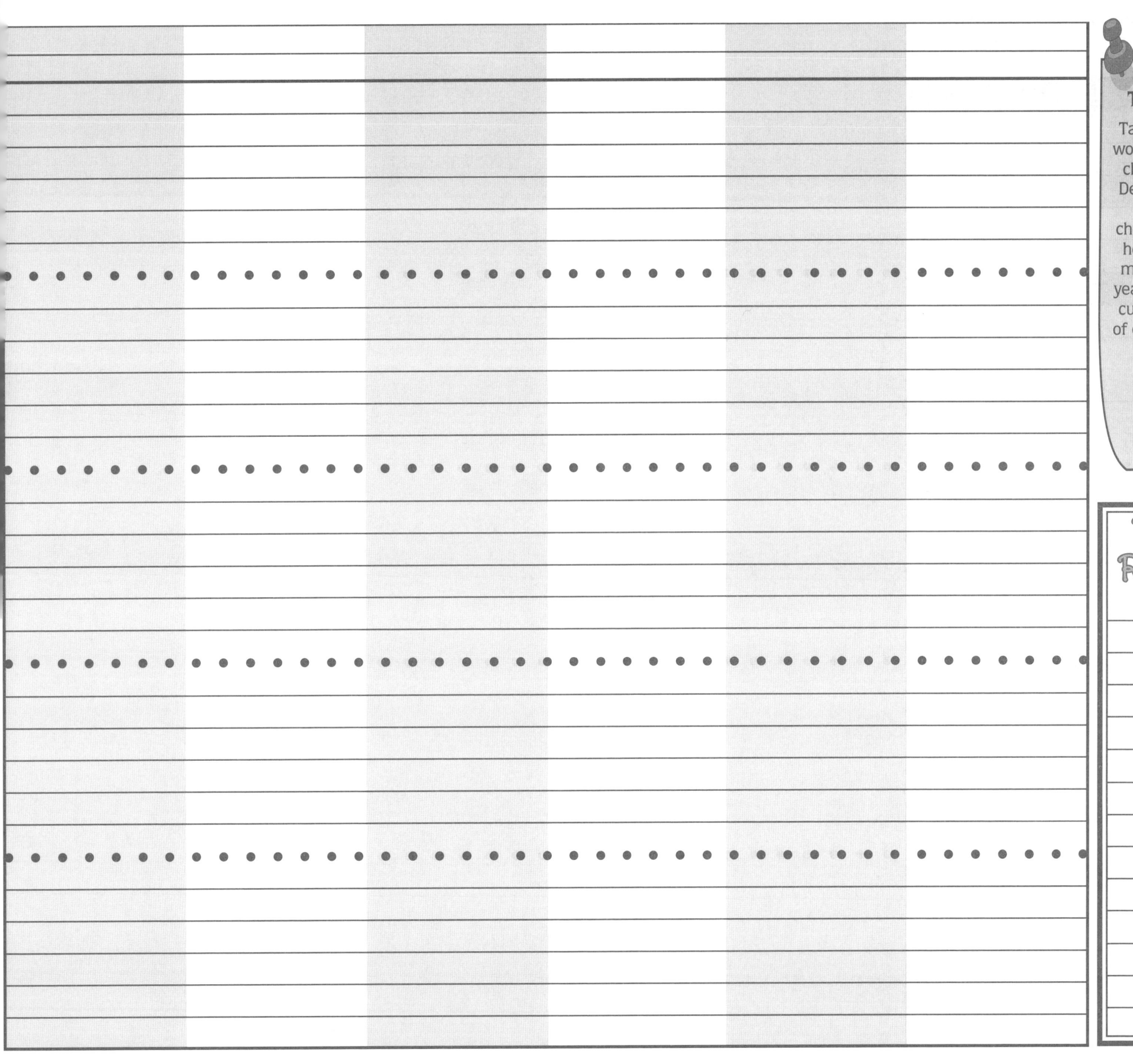

Trip Around the World

Take a virtual trip around the world. Choose or have students choose countries of interest. Depending on the grade level, you may present country choices with brief overviews to help students decide. Once a month throughout the school year, introduce students to the culture, food, geography, etc., of one country with fun lessons and activities. Exploring the world without leaving the classroom can provide students with "passports to learning."

Things to Remember

Week of _____	Subject Time					
Monday Date: Absences:	Take Note					
Tuesday Date: Absences:	Take Note					
Wednesday Date: Absences:	Take Note					
Thursday Date: Absences:	Take Note					
Friday Date: Absences:	Take Note					

What's Your Name?
Preprint extra student name tags—handwritten or computer generated. Having additional name tags on hand will definitely be beneficial to special class teachers (music, art, physical education, etc.) as they learn students' names at the beginning of the year. The extra name tags will also come in handy for field trips, visits from guest speakers, etc.

Things to Remember

Week of _____	Subject _____ Time					
Monday Date: Absences:	Take Note					
Tuesday Date: Absences:	Take Note					
Wednesday Date: Absences:	Take Note					
Thursday Date: Absences:	Take Note					
Friday Date: Absences:	Take Note					

© Carson-Dellosa • CD-104069

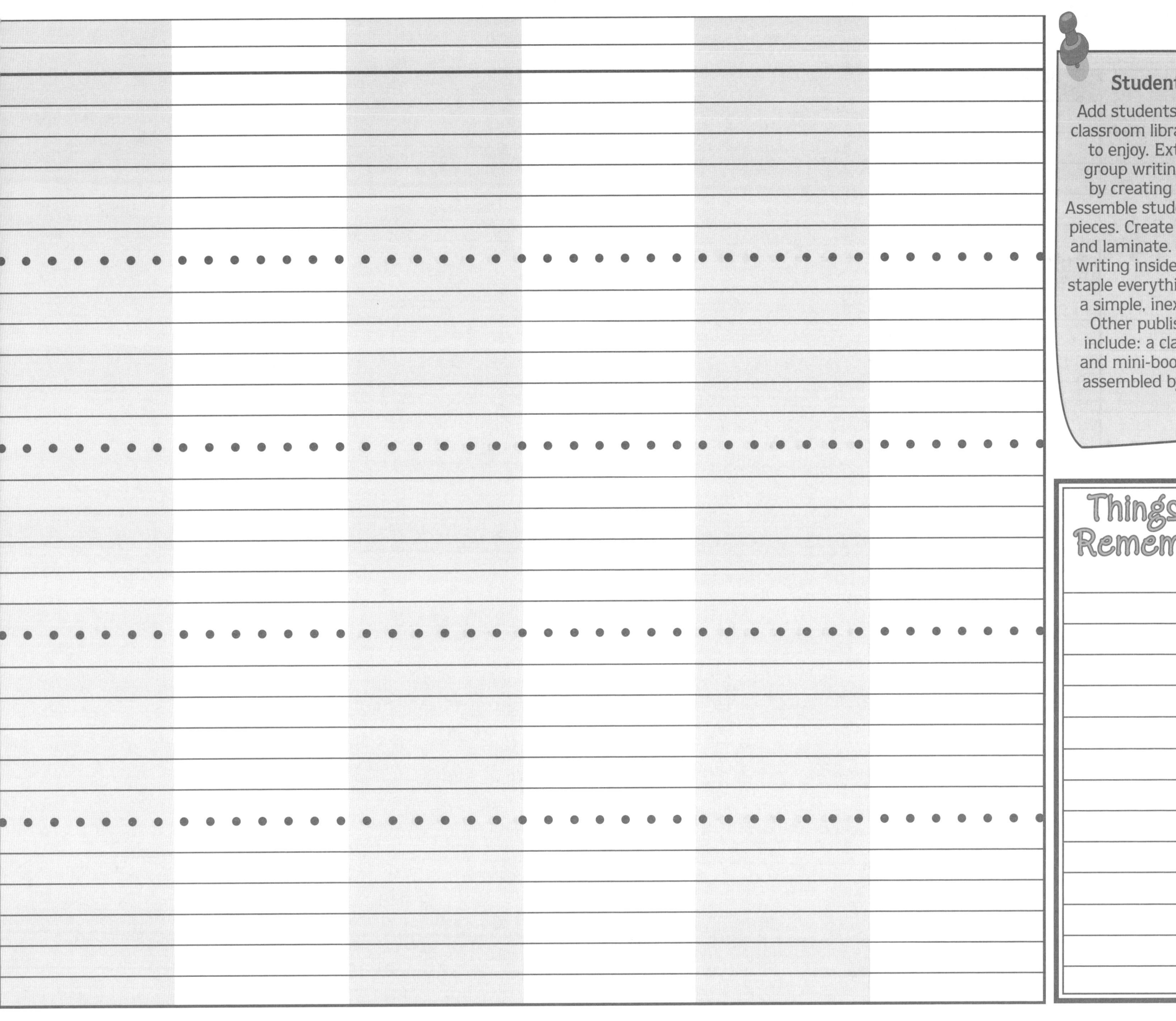

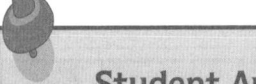

Student Authors

Add students' writing to the classroom library for everyone to enjoy. Extend a whole-group writing assignment by creating a class book. Assemble students' completed pieces. Create a colorful cover and laminate. Place students' writing inside the cover and staple everything together for a simple, inexpensive book. Other publishing options include: a class newspaper and mini-books written and assembled by each student.

Things to Remember

Week of _____	Subject _____ Time						
Monday Date: Absences:	Take Note						
Tuesday Date: Absences:	Take Note						
Wednesday Date: Absences:	Take Note						
Thursday Date: Absences:	Take Note						
Friday Date: Absences:	Take Note						

Listen While You Work

Play various genres of music each morning or during independent work time. Music, depending on the type, can be soothing or a motivating factor for students to complete assignments.

Things to Remember

© Carson-Dellosa • CD-104069

Week of _____	Subject Time					
Monday Date: Absences:	Take Note					
Tuesday Date: Absences:	Take Note					
Wednesday Date: Absences:	Take Note					
Thursday Date: Absences:	Take Note					
Friday Date: Absences:	Take Note					

Desk Refresher

Revitalize student desks by replacing desk nameplates after winter break. Desk nameplates can get tattered or torn over the course of the school year. Simply change desk nameplates after winter break. Students will feel like their work areas are totally new spaces.

Things to Remember

Week of _____	Subject Time						
Monday Date: Absences:	Take Note						
Tuesday Date: Absences:	Take Note						
Wednesday Date: Absences:	Take Note						
Thursday Date: Absences:	Take Note						
Friday Date: Absences:	Take Note						

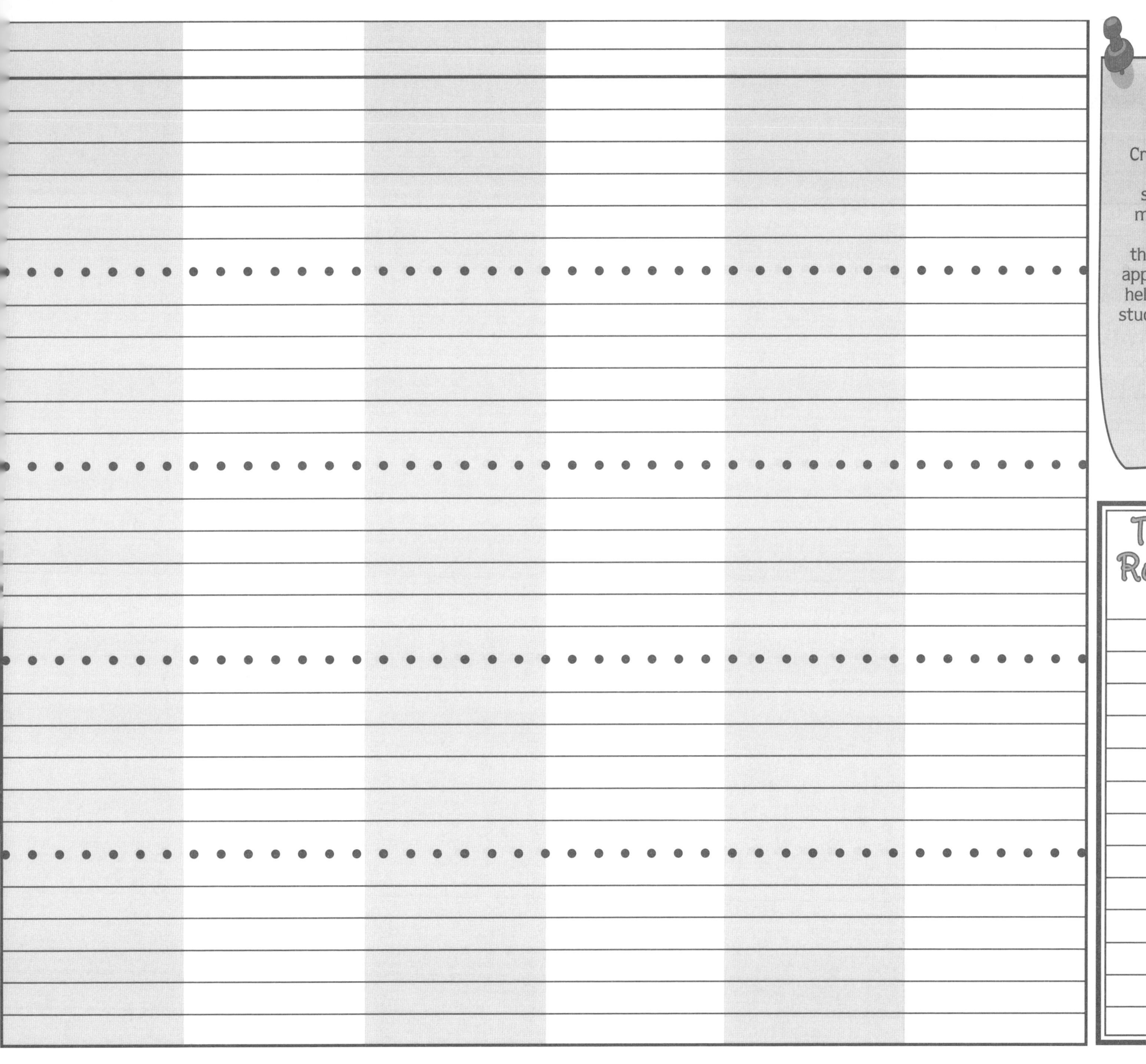

Student Tips

Create practical resources for students. Study skills, testing tips, and multiplication tables are all helpful reminders that students will greatly appreciate. Simply copy any helpful resources and have students place them in their notebooks or folders for reference.

Things to Remember

Week of _____	Subject Time					
Monday Date: Absences:	Take Note					
Tuesday Date: Absences:	Take Note					
Wednesday Date: Absences:	Take Note					
Thursday Date: Absences:	Take Note					
Friday Date: Absences:	Take Note					

© Carson-Dellosa • CD-104069

In Case You're Away

Create a substitute teacher lesson plan template—handwritten or computer generated. The template will save you time and energy. Include lessons for each subject, a list of reliable students, a section for free time or fun activities, etc. Whether you are planning for a scheduled absence or making sure you are prepared for any unexpected absences, simply fill in the template with specific instructions for your substitute.

Things to Remember

Week of _____	Subject Time					
Monday Date: Absences:	Take Note					
Tuesday Date: Absences:	Take Note					
Wednesday Date: Absences:	Take Note					
Thursday Date: Absences:	Take Note					
Friday Date: Absences:	Take Note					

© Carson-Dellosa • CD-104069

Certification Renewal Information

Organize your teaching certification renewal requirements or continuing education information with a few simple steps. Create a binder for storing continuing education requirements, course information, and completion certificates. When your teaching certification is due for renewal, you will have all of your important information in one location.

Things to Remember

Week of _____	Subject Time					
Monday Date: Absences:	Take Note					
Tuesday Date: Absences:	Take Note					
Wednesday Date: Absences:	Take Note					
Thursday Date: Absences:	Take Note					
Friday Date: Absences:	Take Note					

© Carson-Dellosa • CD-104069

Teacher Scrapbook

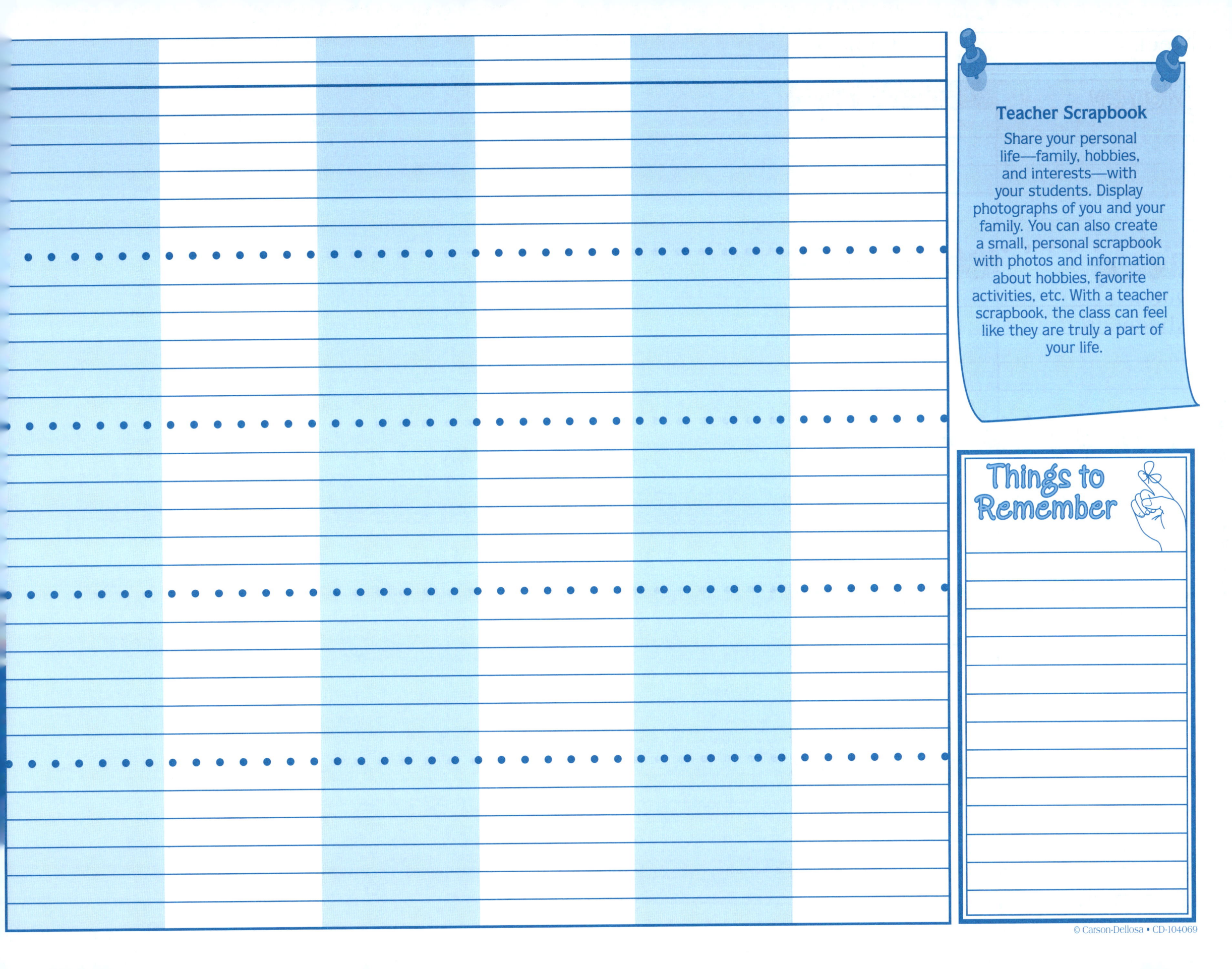

Share your personal life—family, hobbies, and interests—with your students. Display photographs of you and your family. You can also create a small, personal scrapbook with photos and information about hobbies, favorite activities, etc. With a teacher scrapbook, the class can feel like they are truly a part of your life.

Things to Remember

Week of _____	Subject _____ Time					
Monday Date: Absences:	Take Note					
Tuesday Date: Absences:	Take Note					
Wednesday Date: Absences:	Take Note					
Thursday Date: Absences:	Take Note					
Friday Date: Absences:	Take Note					

Lining Up to Review

Usually, students line up when exiting the classroom, whether they are going for a short trip to the library or leaving for the day. Make lining up a fun, teachable moment by reviewing curriculum concepts as students are called to line up. Ask each student a curriculum question (math fact, grammar rule, etc.) and allow him to line up only after the question has been answered correctly. If you are pressed for time, allow groups of students to collaborate on the answers, then line up together.

Things to Remember

Week of _____	Subject Time					
Monday Date: Absences:	Take Note					
Tuesday Date: Absences:	Take Note					
Wednesday Date: Absences:	Take Note					
Thursday Date: Absences:	Take Note					
Friday Date: Absences:	Take Note					

© Carson-Dellosa • CD-104069

Games as Review

Play a simple game with the class to review curriculum concepts by turning important content into answers to game-show-type questions. Split students into two teams. Have students come up with questions that match the given answers. Examples include: "Raleigh; What is the capital of North Carolina?" and "noun; What is a person, place, or thing?" Reviewing concepts or preparing for upcoming tests has never been so fun!

Things to Remember

Week of _____	Subject Time						
Monday Date: Absences:	Take Note						
Tuesday Date: Absences:	Take Note						
Wednesday Date: Absences:	Take Note						
Thursday Date: Absences:	Take Note						
Friday Date: Absences:	Take Note						

© Carson-Dellosa • CD-104069

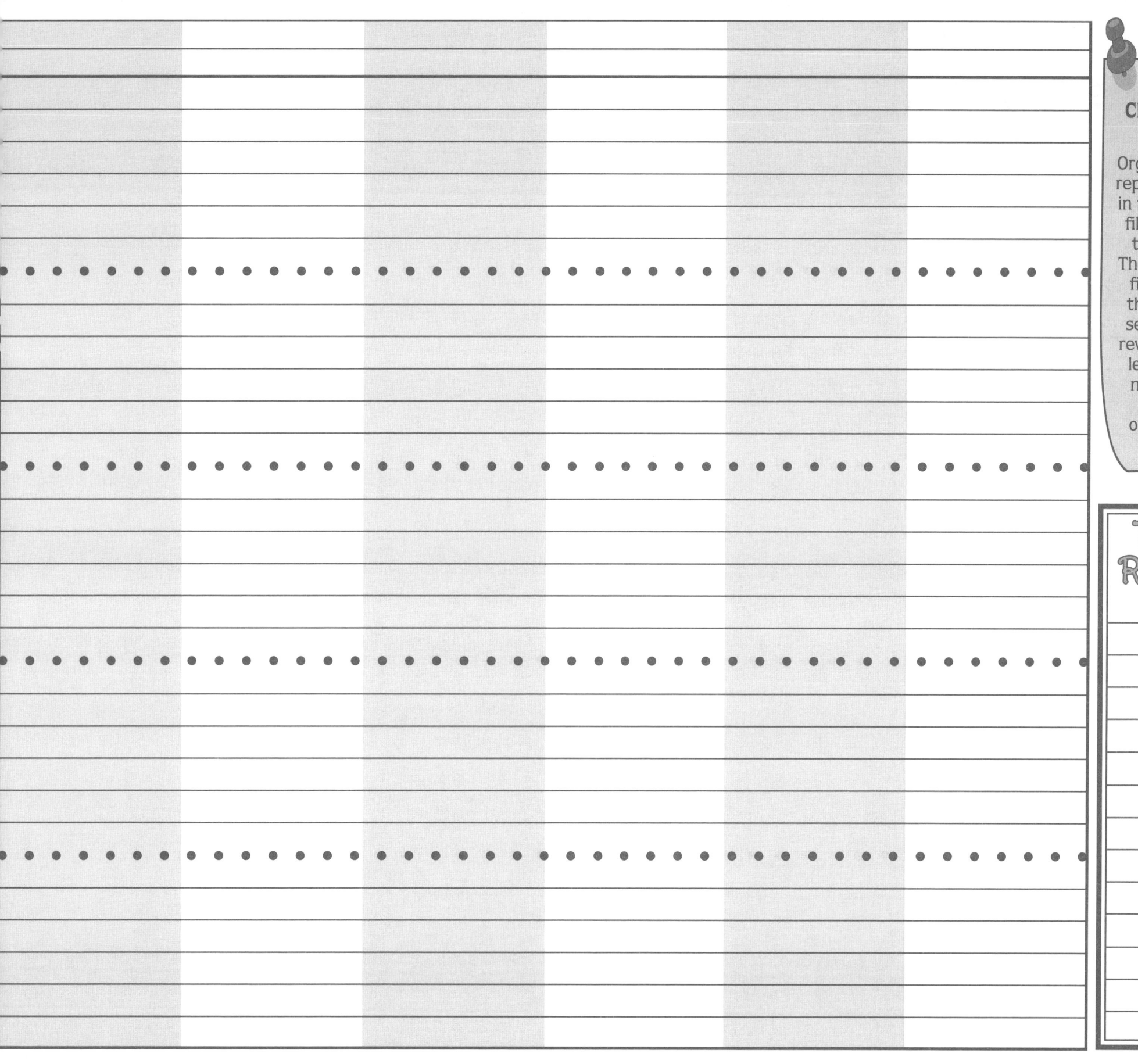

Classroom Organization Made Simple

Organize all of your classroom reproducibles by placing them in file folders. Sort, label, and file reproducibles according to theme or subject area. Then, arrange folders in your filing system according to the time of year (month or season) that the concept is reviewed or taught. Planning lessons will be much more manageable since student activity sheets will be organized and easy to find.

Things to Remember

Week of _____	Subject Time					
Monday Date: Absences:	Take Note					
Tuesday Date: Absences:	Take Note					
Wednesday Date: Absences:	Take Note					
Thursday Date: Absences:	Take Note					
Friday Date: Absences:	Take Note					

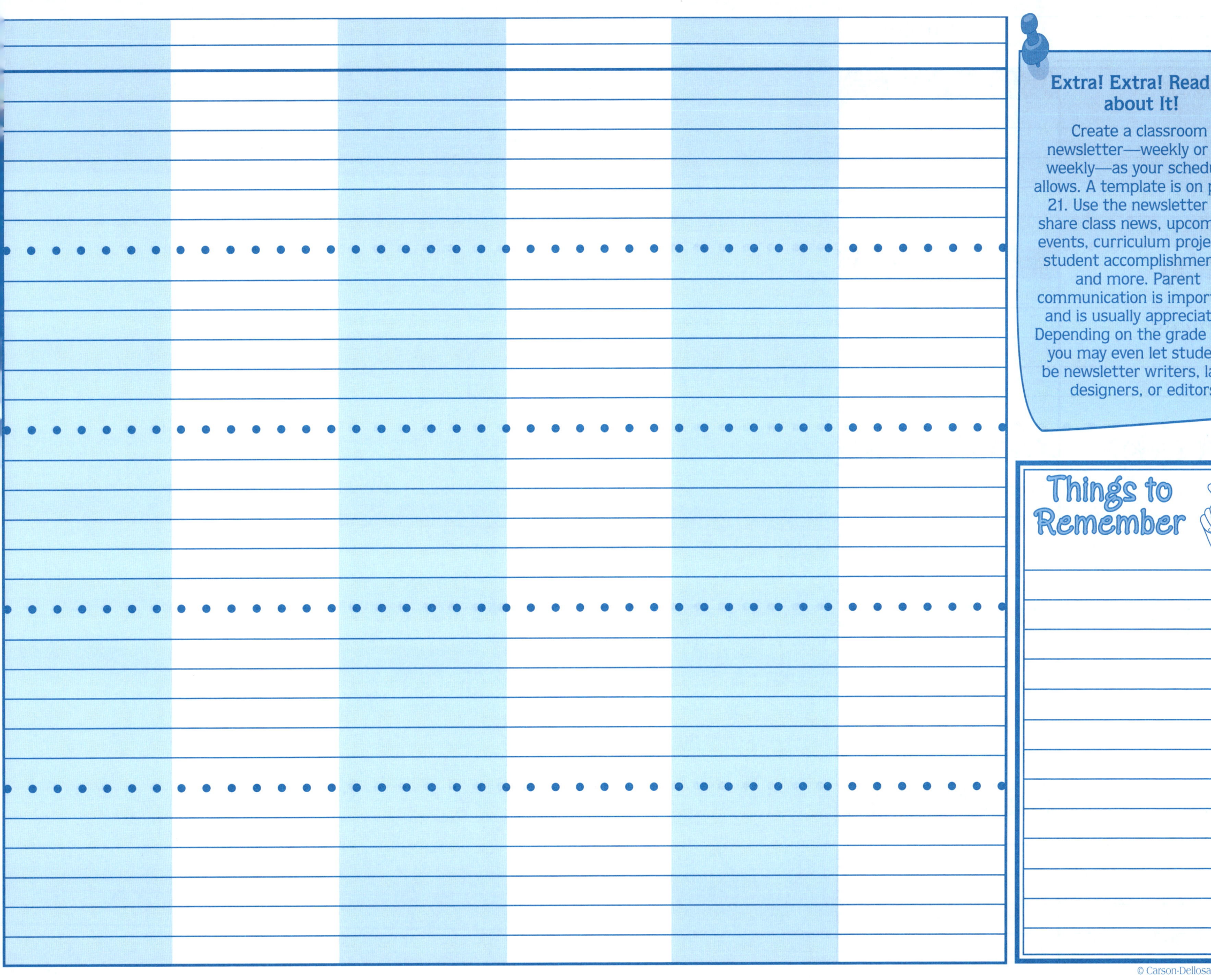

Extra! Extra! Read All about It!

Create a classroom newsletter—weekly or bi-weekly—as your schedule allows. A template is on page 21. Use the newsletter to share class news, upcoming events, curriculum projects, student accomplishments, and more. Parent communication is important and is usually appreciated. Depending on the grade level, you may even let students be newsletter writers, layout designers, or editors.

Things to Remember

Week of _____	Subject Time					
Monday Date: Absences:	Take Note					
Tuesday Date: Absences:	Take Note					
Wednesday Date: Absences:	Take Note					
Thursday Date: Absences:	Take Note					
Friday Date: Absences:	Take Note					

Field Trips Galore

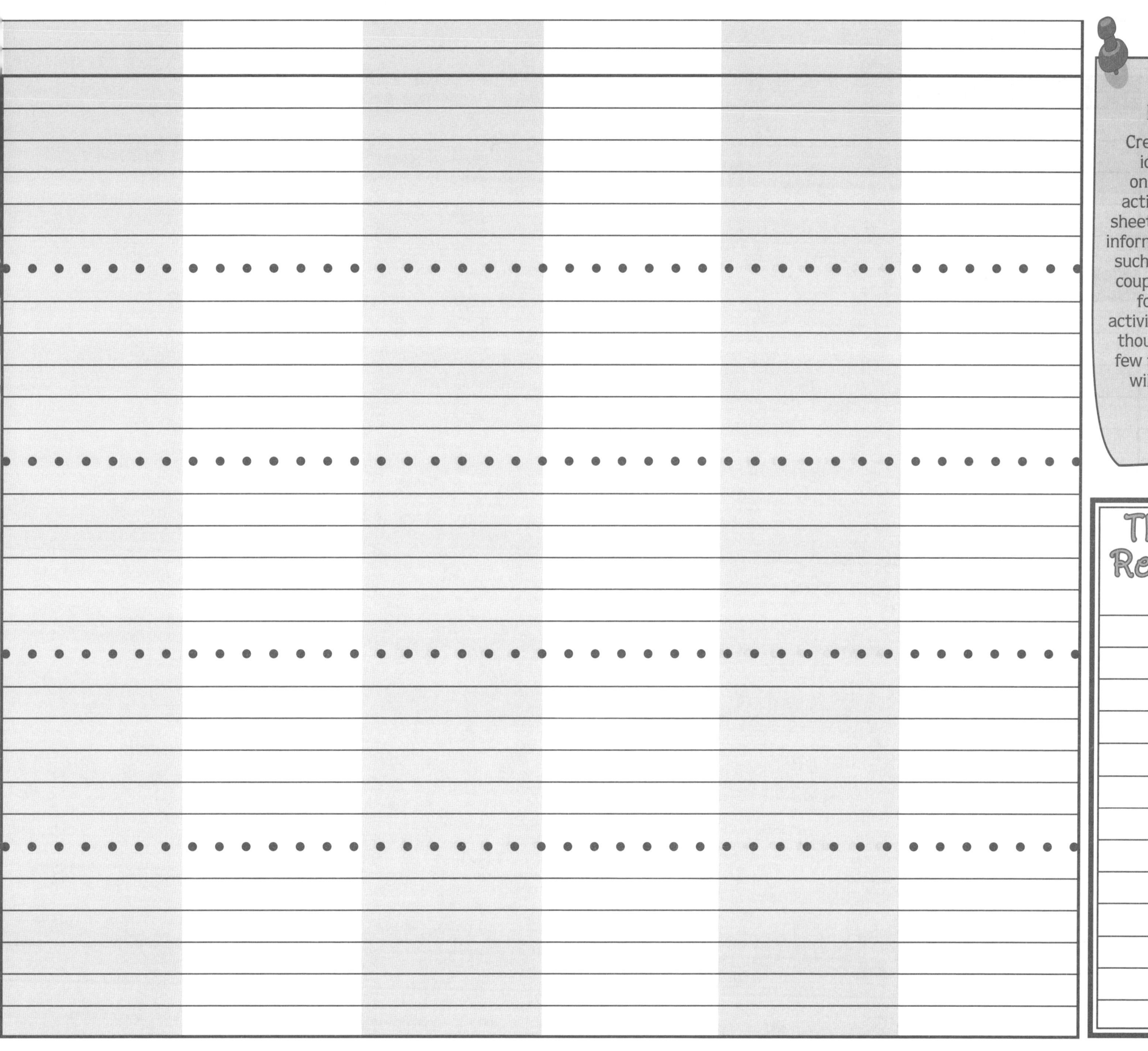

Create a binder filled with ideas and information on field trips and special activities. Use clear plastic sheet protectors to store the information. Include materials such as brochures, discount coupons, and creative ideas for curriculum-related activities and field trips. Even though you may only take a few field trips each year, you will accumulate plenty of ideas for future use.

Things to Remember

	Subject					
Week of _____	Time					
Monday Date: Absences:	Take Note					
Tuesday Date: Absences:	Take Note					
Wednesday Date: Absences:	Take Note					
Thursday Date: Absences:	Take Note					
Friday Date: Absences:	Take Note					

© Carson-Dellosa • CD-104069

Family Night

Plan a special family night during each grading period. Organize activities such as popular board games, science experiments, curriculum-related bingo, and more. Family nights help extend communication between you and parents and foster the relationships between students and their parents. Creating a classroom community provides opportunities for teamwork and can help you have a successful school year.

Things to Remember

Week of _____	Subject Time						
Monday Date: Absences:	Take Note						
Tuesday Date: Absences:	Take Note						
Wednesday Date: Absences:	Take Note						
Thursday Date: Absences:	Take Note						
Friday Date: Absences:	Take Note						

© Carson-Dellosa • CD-104069

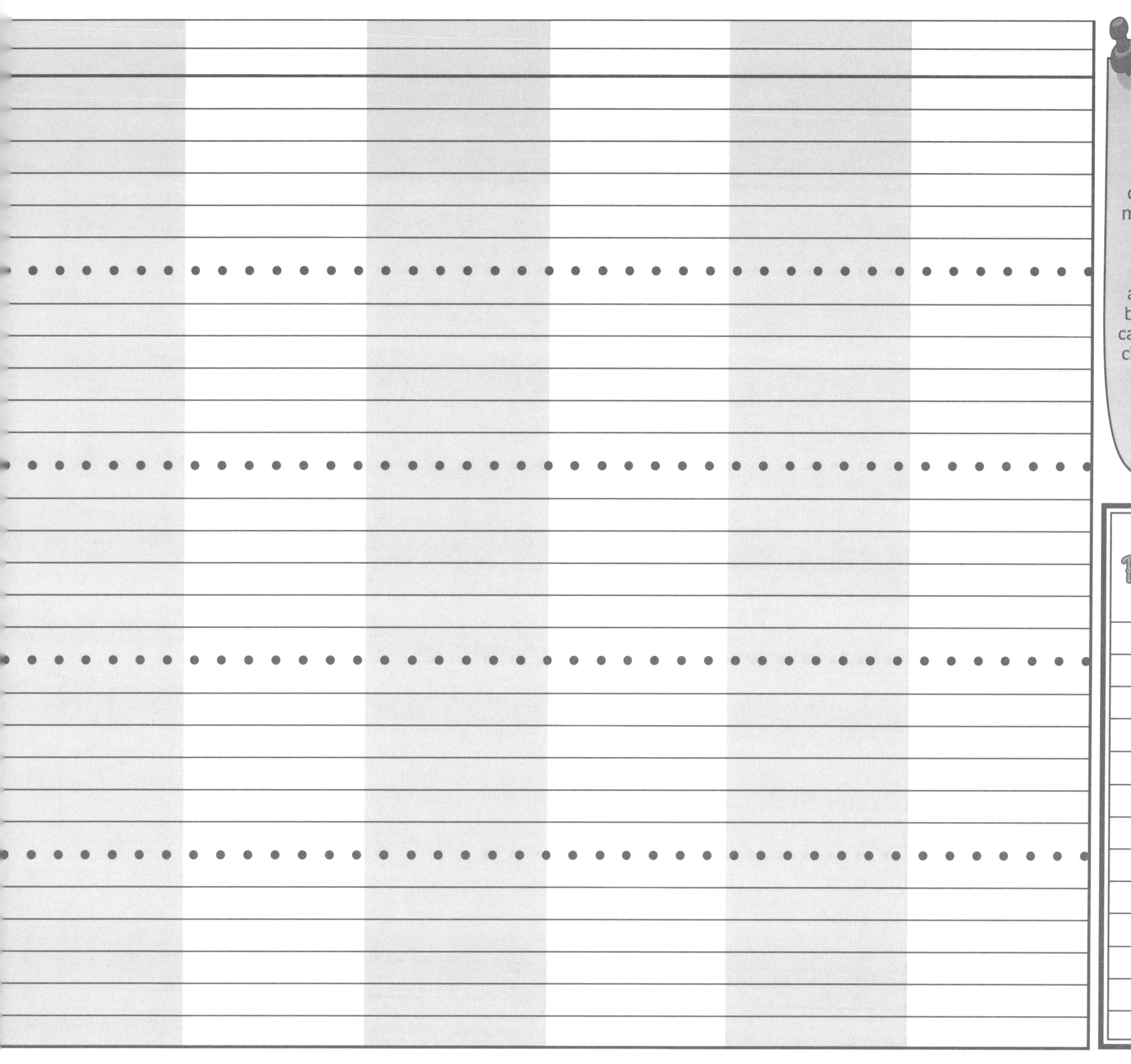

Calendar Management

Create a simple organizational tool for your calendar materials. Store calendar cover-ups for each month in a small plastic bag. Record the corresponding month on each bag with a permanent marker or use an adhesive label. Store the bags in a container near the calendar display. Whether you choose to have daily calendar activities or simply use the calendar as a reference display, the pieces will be organized and easy to use.

Things to Remember

Week of _____	Subject Time						
Monday Date: Absences:	Take Note						
Tuesday Date: Absences:	Take Note						
Wednesday Date: Absences:	Take Note						
Thursday Date: Absences:	Take Note						
Friday Date: Absences:	Take Note						

© Carson-Dellosa • CD-10406

Classroom IDs

Use student photographs to help you, substitute teachers, class volunteers, special class teachers, and others know important information about students. Take photographs of students and glue the photos on index cards. On the backs of the cards, record important information, such as students' names and emergency contact phone numbers. Store the cards in a recipe or file card box and place in a central location.

Things to Remember

Week of _____	Subject Time						
Monday Date: Absences:	Take Note						
Tuesday Date: Absences:	Take Note						
Wednesday Date: Absences:	Take Note						
Thursday Date: Absences:	Take Note						
Friday Date: Absences:	Take Note						

Parent To-Do List

Save time by keeping a current to-do list with specific instructions for parents and other classroom volunteers. You can also keep a list or folder of tasks for volunteer parents to complete at home. Some examples are cutting, coloring, word processing, collating, stapling, etc. When parents and other volunteers are ready to help, you will have tasks ready to give them.

Things to Remember

Week of _____	Subject Time					
Monday Date: Absences:	Take Note					
Tuesday Date: Absences:	Take Note					
Wednesday Date: Absences:	Take Note					
Thursday Date: Absences:	Take Note					
Friday Date: Absences:	Take Note					

Student Dictionaries

It is important for students to have access to reference materials. Create personal student dictionaries by trimming 8 ½" x 11" (22 cm x 28 cm) paper to 5" x 8" (13 cm x 20 cm). Cut and staple together enough paper for each student to have 52 pages—two pages per letter of the alphabet. Staple the paper along the left sides to make books. Each time a student needs to spell a word or find a definition, have her write the correct spelling of the word and the definition in her student dictionary. This lets each student create a useful reference of her own.

Things to Remember

Week of _____	Subject Time					
Monday Date: Absences:	Take Note					
Tuesday Date: Absences:	Take Note					
Wednesday Date: Absences:	Take Note					
Thursday Date: Absences:	Take Note					
Friday Date: Absences:	Take Note					

Classroom Library Under Construction

There are many ways to build a classroom library. Some can be quite expensive, while others are be quite thrifty. Ask students to bring book donations—new or used—from home, with their parents' permission. Raise money to purchase books using bake sales, lemonade stands, car washes, etc. Utilize book clubs for great discounts. Sometimes book club book prices are relatively inexpensive, and you can also earn points to receive free books. Visit used bookstores, garage/yard sales, and flea markets for ultimate deals. Your classroom library will be complete in no time!

Things to Remember

Week of _____	Subject Time						
Monday Date: Absences:	Take Note						
Tuesday Date: Absences:	Take Note						
Wednesday Date: Absences:	Take Note						
Thursday Date: Absences:	Take Note						
Friday Date: Absences:	Take Note						

© Carson-Dellosa • CD-104069

Open House with Pizzazz

An open house provides an opportunity for parents to learn information, explore the classroom, view students' work, etc. Some open houses have set schedules with planned agendas, while others are "floating" events, with parents coming and going when they can. Whatever the format, an open house does not have to be scheduled at the beginning of the school year. Use an open house as a means of sharing a class project, holding a play or skit, or even just gathering for the fun of it. Holding regularly scheduled open houses can help to create a wonderful sense of classroom community.

Things to Remember

Week of _____	Subject Time					
Monday Date: Absences:	Take Note					
Tuesday Date: Absences:	Take Note					
Wednesday Date: Absences:	Take Note					
Thursday Date: Absences:	Take Note					
Friday Date: Absences:	Take Note					

© Carson-Dellosa • CD-10406

Meaningful Motivators

Remember that words of encouragement can make all the difference. Comments such as, "Good job," "You made a difference," and "You're amazing," can be just what students need for motivation. Sometimes it is easy to make negative comments, so make it a priority to share positive thoughts with your students.

Things to Remember

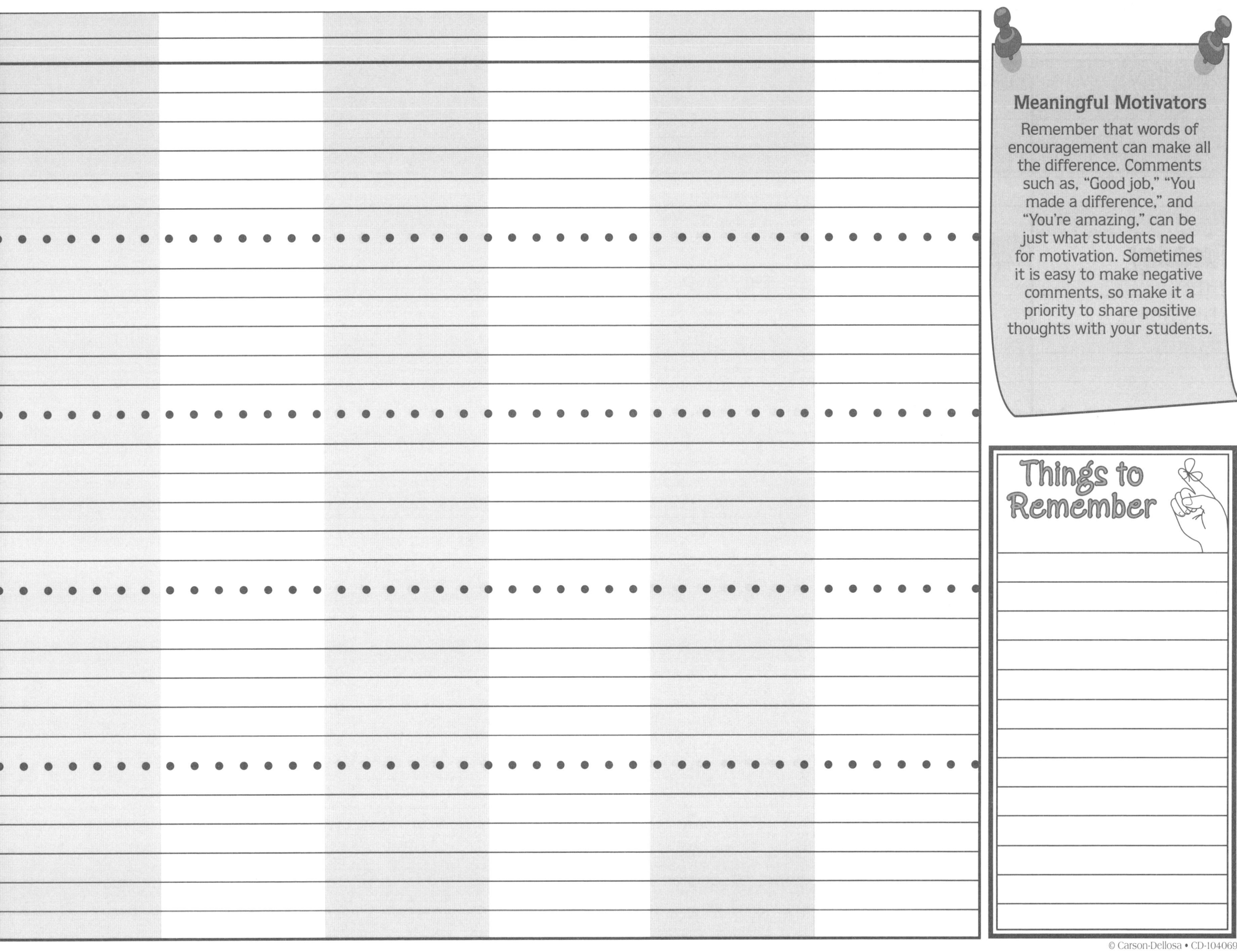

Week of _____	Subject _____ Time					
Monday Date: Absences:	Take Note					
Tuesday Date: Absences:	Take Note					
Wednesday Date: Absences:	Take Note					
Thursday Date: Absences:	Take Note					
Friday Date: Absences:	Take Note					

© Carson-Dellosa • CD-104069

Birthday Celebrations

Celebrating all of the birthdays of your students can be overwhelming. Make each student feel special by having the rest of the class create a birthday book for him. When a student birthday rolls around, have classmates write birthday wishes or stories for the birthday student. Make sure classmates include illustrations to go with their writing. Use the computer to create a simple cover, then mount it on construction paper and laminate. Finally, staple the pages and cover together and present it to the birthday student. Classroom-created treasures will brighten any birthday.

Things to Remember

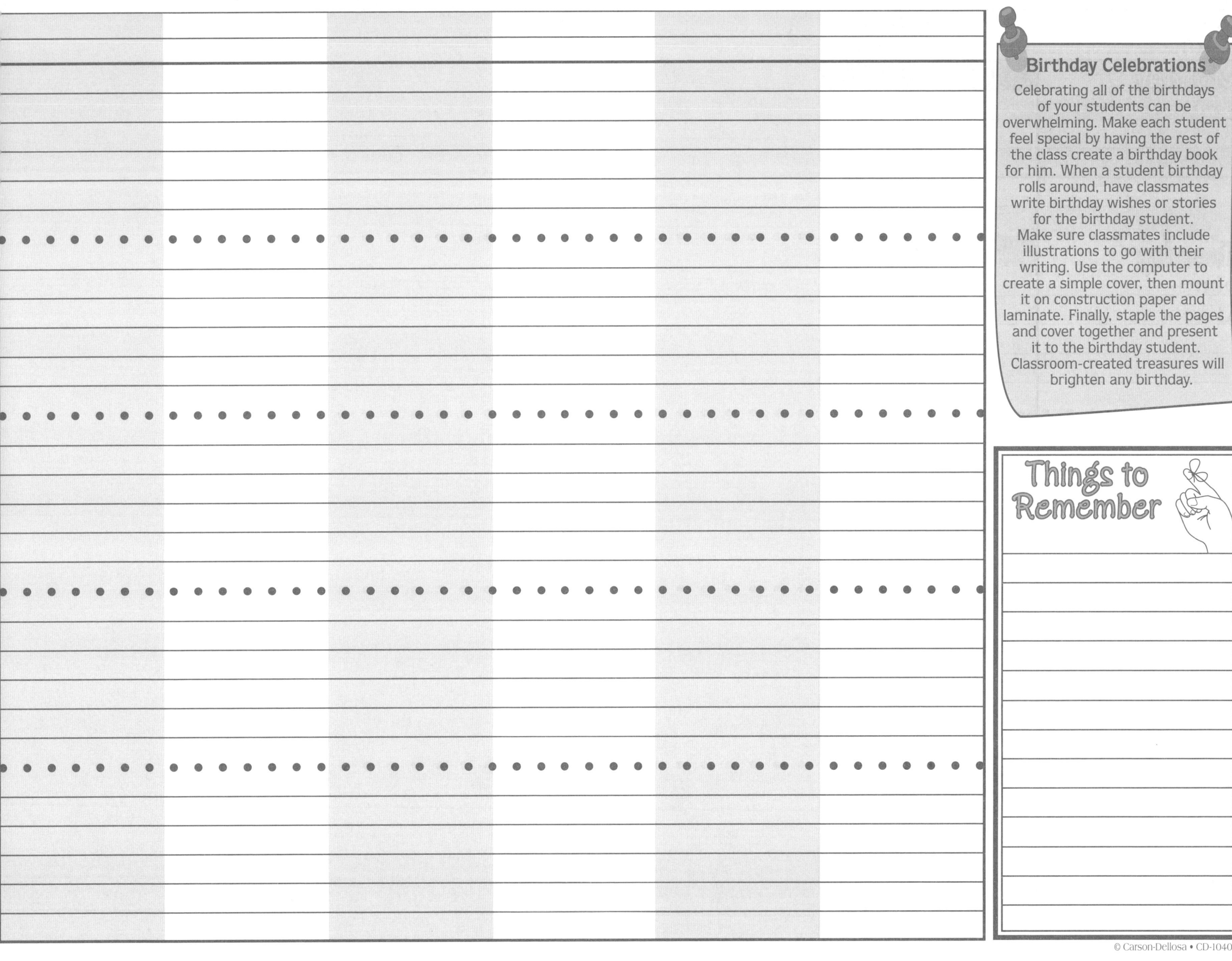

Week of _____	Subject					
	Time					
Monday Date: Absences:	Take Note					
Tuesday Date: Absences:	Take Note					
Wednesday Date: Absences:	Take Note					
Thursday Date: Absences:	Take Note					
Friday Date: Absences:	Take Note					

© Carson-Dellosa • CD-104069

Morning Work Organization

Organize morning work for the school year in a three-ring binder. Each week, make copies of the reproducibles or activities you will use each morning. As lessons plans become more complicated each week, this simple task will definitely come in handy and is useful for substitutes, as well. Use clear, plastic sheet protectors to extend the life of your binder materials.

Things to Remember

Week of _____	Subject Time					
Monday Date: Absences:	Take Note					
Tuesday Date: Absences:	Take Note					
Wednesday Date: Absences:	Take Note					
Thursday Date: Absences:	Take Note					
Friday Date: Absences:	Take Note					

© Carson-Dellosa • CD-104069

Minus the Roll Call

Track attendance and foster student responsibility without the traditional roll call. Write each student's name in red on one side of an index card, then in black on the other side. Place the cards in a pocket chart near the classroom door. Be sure that the sides with their names in red are showing. As students arrive each morning, have them turn their cards to the black sides. With a quick glance, you will be able to determine the students who are absent for the day, based on the color of their names. Each afternoon, have a student volunteer turn the cards to the red sides for the next day's attendance procedure. It may take a couple of weeks for students to turn their cards without a reminder, but it will be well worth the effort.

Things to Remember

Week of _____	Subject Time					
Monday Date: Absences:	Take Note					
Tuesday Date: Absences:	Take Note					
Wednesday Date: Absences:	Take Note					
Thursday Date: Absences:	Take Note					
Friday Date: Absences:	Take Note					

Literature Shared

Share an extra bit of literature each day. Regardless of the grade level you teach, reading aloud to your students is priceless for them. Read approximately 10-15 minutes each day. Choose a chapter book, making sure to choose a title or subject of interest to your students. Students enjoy being read to, and it strengthens their fluency skills as well as their love and enjoyment of reading.

Things to Remember

Week of _____	Subject Time					
Monday Date: Absences:	Take Note					
Tuesday Date: Absences:	Take Note					
Wednesday Date: Absences:	Take Note					
Thursday Date: Absences:	Take Note					
Friday Date: Absences:	Take Note					

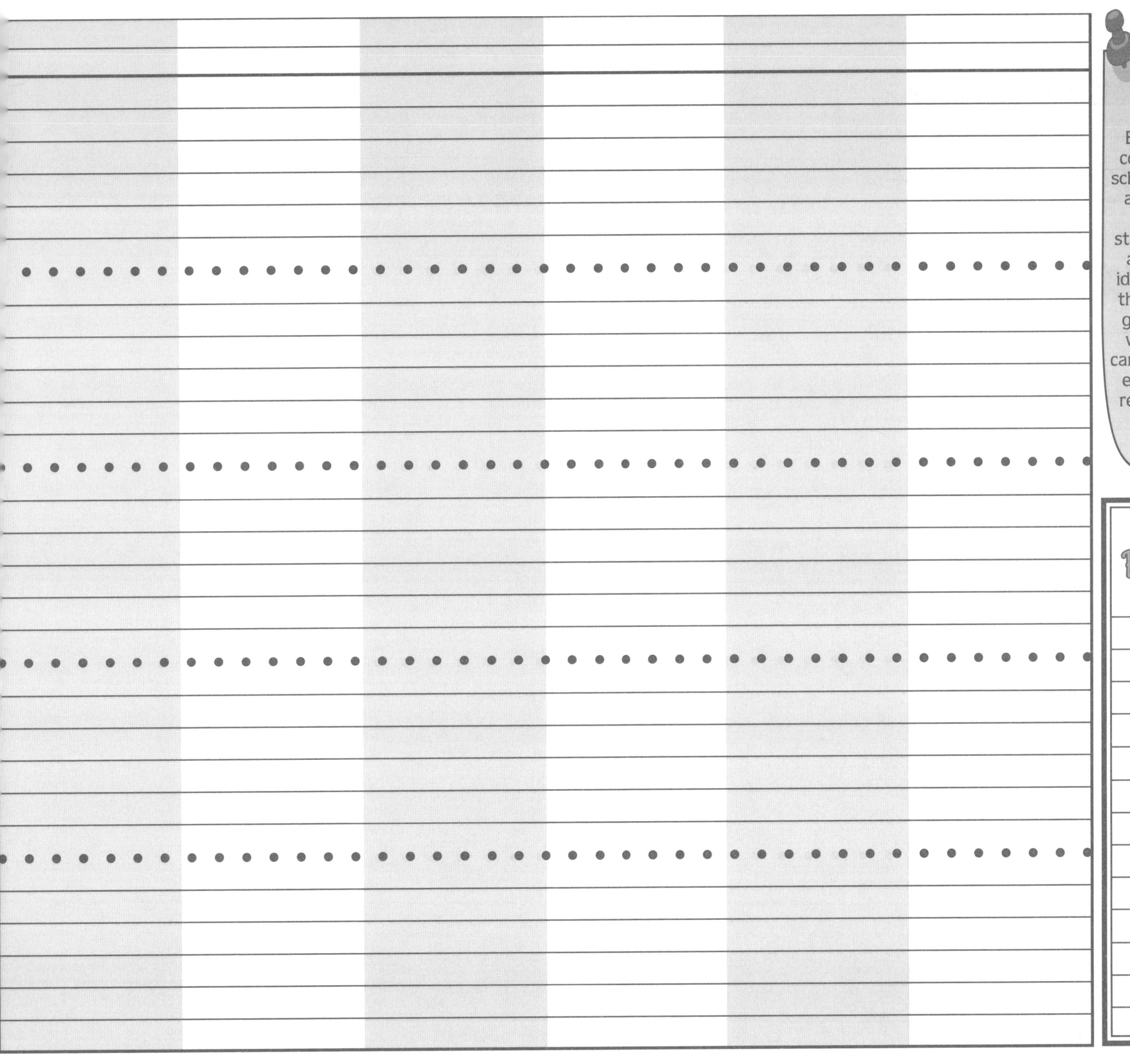

Extra Activities for Fast Workers

Be prepared when students complete their work ahead of schedule. Keep a folder of extra activities—those that foster critical thinking skills—for students who finish their class assignments early. Another idea is to designate an area in the classroom for students to go when they complete their work. In this area, students can treat themselves by playing educational games silently or reading books once their work is complete!

Things to Remember

Week of _____	Subject _____ Time					
Monday Date: Absences:	Take Note					
Tuesday Date: Absences:	Take Note					
Wednesday Date: Absences:	Take Note					
Thursday Date: Absences:	Take Note					
Friday Date: Absences:	Take Note					

© Carson-Dellosa • CD-104069

Transition Time

Sometimes, transitions between activities or lessons do not go quite as smoothly as desired, so plan for them. Include fun transition activities in your daily lesson planning, especially for transition times that could become lengthy. For example, an art activity may take longer than scheduled because students complete projects and clean-up at different times. Use a variety of transition activities (math challenges, sentence starters, word puzzles, etc.).

Things to Remember

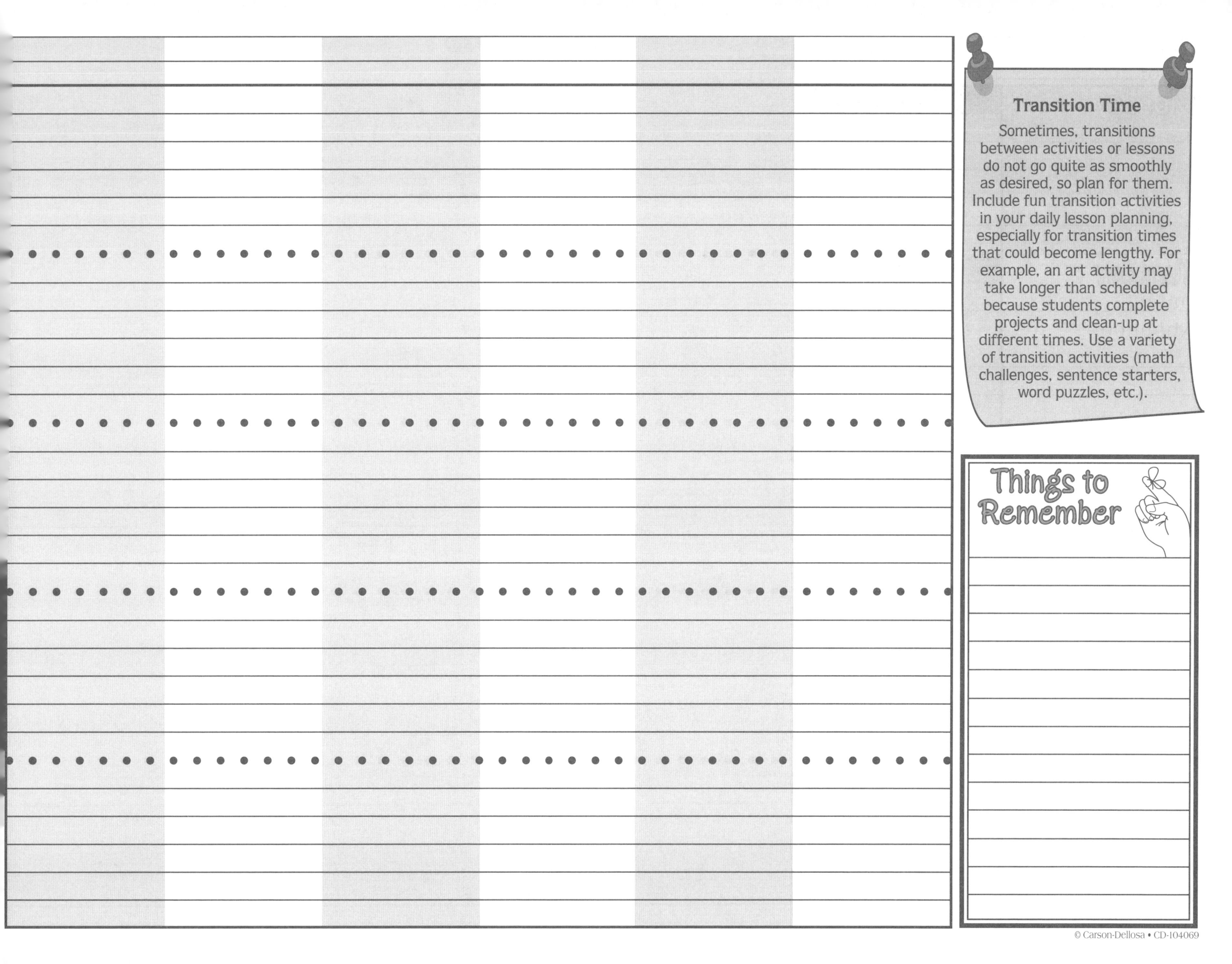

Week of _____	Subject Time					
Monday Date: Absences:	Take Note					
Tuesday Date: Absences:	Take Note					
Wednesday Date: Absences:	Take Note					
Thursday Date: Absences:	Take Note					
Friday Date: Absences:	Take Note					

While You Were Out

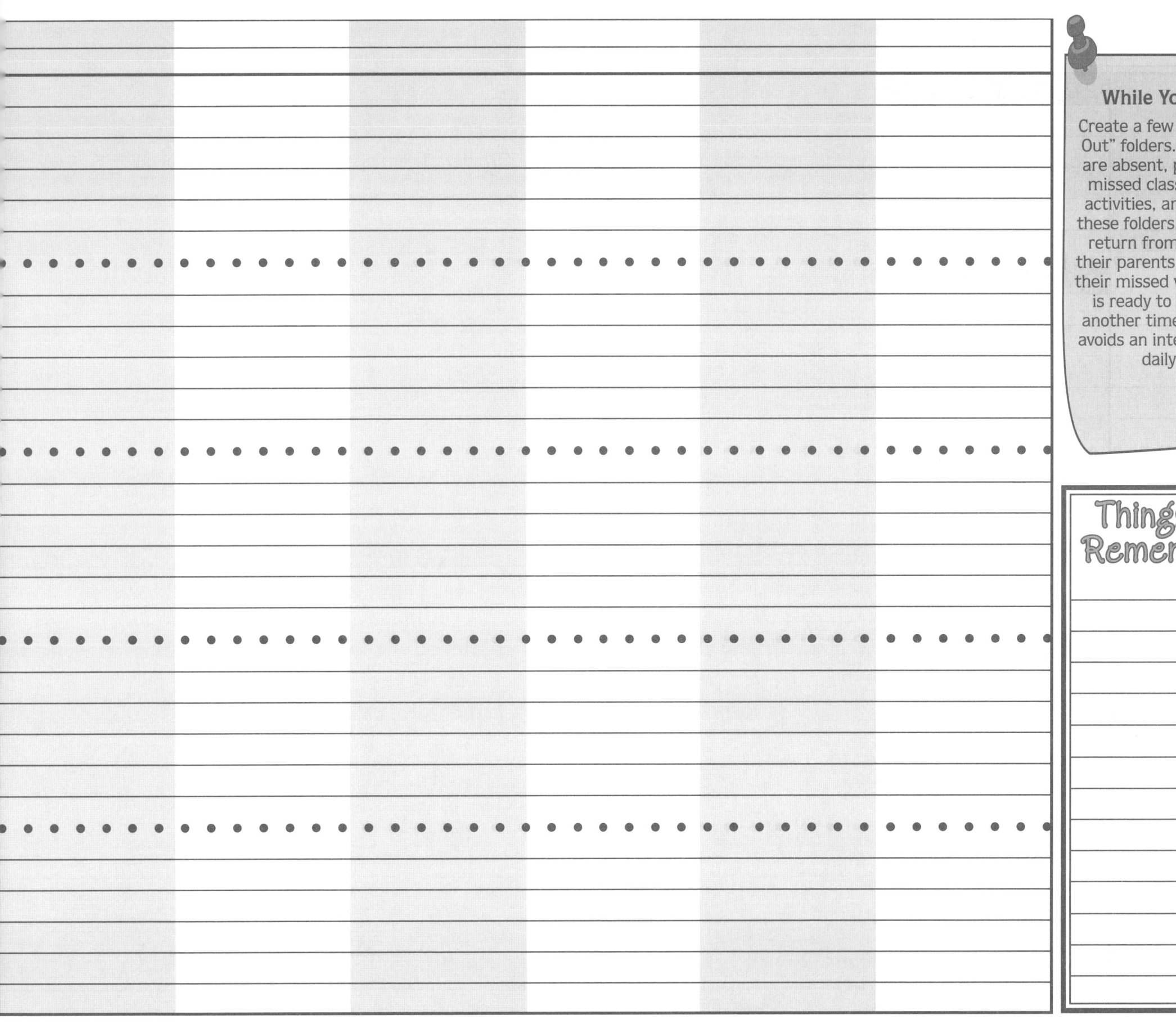

Create a few "While You Were Out" folders. When students are absent, place all of their missed class assignments, activities, and homework in these folders. When students return from absences or if their parents come to pick up their missed work, everything is ready to go. This is just another time-saving tip that avoids an interruption to your daily routine.

Things to Remember

Week of _____	Subject Time					
Monday Date: Absences:	Take Note					
Tuesday Date: Absences:	Take Note					
Wednesday Date: Absences:	Take Note					
Thursday Date: Absences:	Take Note					
Friday Date: Absences:	Take Note					

© Carson-Dellosa • CD-104069

Prepared for Parent Conferences

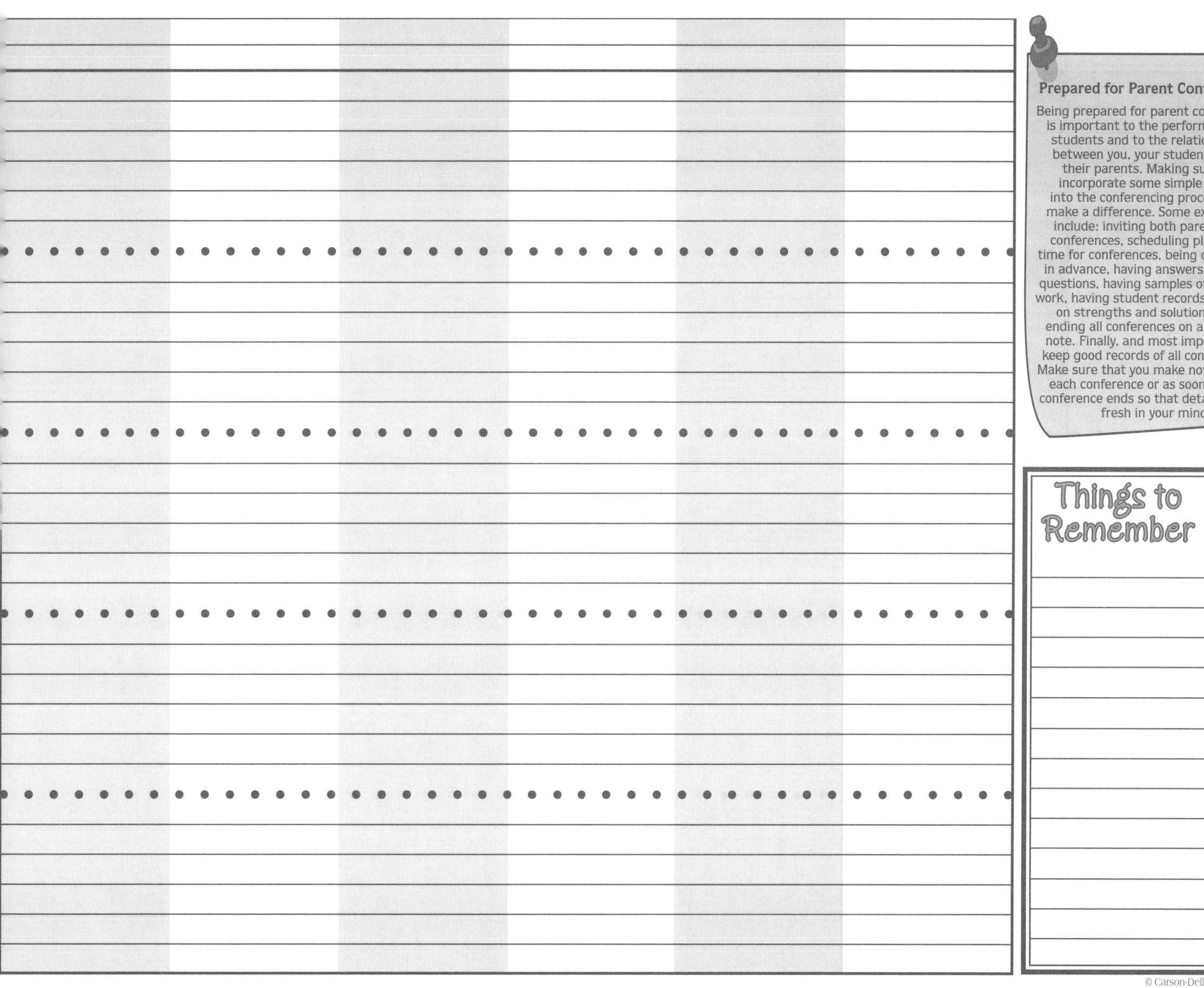

Being prepared for parent conferences is important to the performance of students and to the relationships between you, your students, and their parents. Making sure to incorporate some simple steps into the conferencing process can make a difference. Some examples include: inviting both parents to conferences, scheduling plenty of time for conferences, being organized in advance, having answers to likely questions, having samples of student work, having student records, focusing on strengths and solutions, and ending all conferences on a positive note. Finally, and most importantly, keep good records of all conferences. Make sure that you make notes during each conference or as soon as each conference ends so that details remain fresh in your mind.

Things to Remember

© Carson-Dellosa • CD-104069

Week of _____	Subject Time					
Monday Date: Absences:	Take Note					
Tuesday Date: Absences:	Take Note					
Wednesday Date: Absences:	Take Note					
Thursday Date: Absences:	Take Note					
Friday Date: Absences:	Take Note					

© Carson-Dellosa • CD-104069

Planning for All Learners

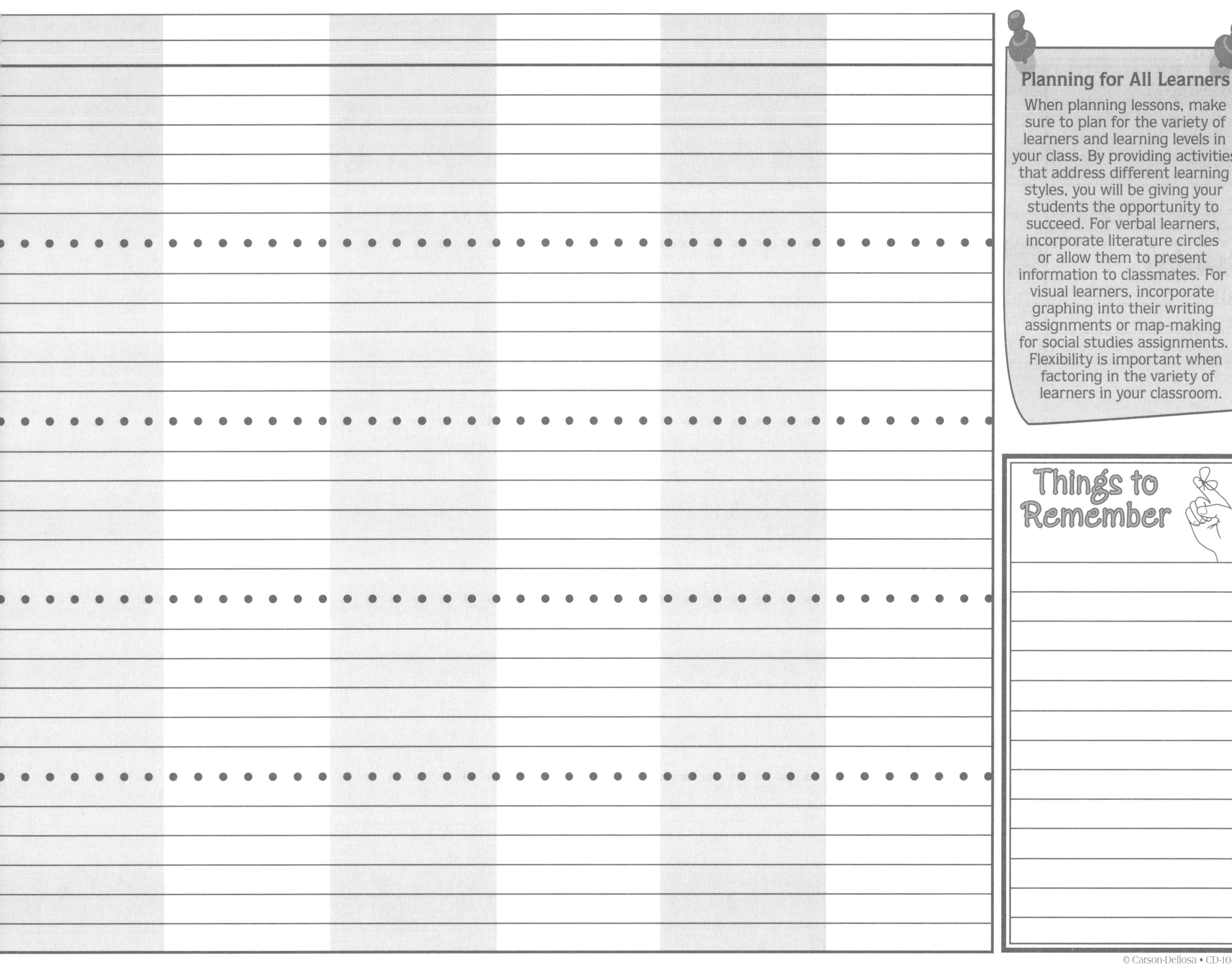

When planning lessons, make sure to plan for the variety of learners and learning levels in your class. By providing activities that address different learning styles, you will be giving your students the opportunity to succeed. For verbal learners, incorporate literature circles or allow them to present information to classmates. For visual learners, incorporate graphing into their writing assignments or map-making for social studies assignments. Flexibility is important when factoring in the variety of learners in your classroom.

Things to Remember

Week of _____	Subject Time					
Monday Date: Absences:	Take Note					
Tuesday Date: Absences:	Take Note					
Wednesday Date: Absences:	Take Note					
Thursday Date: Absences:	Take Note					
Friday Date: Absences:	Take Note					

© Carson-Dellosa • CD-104069

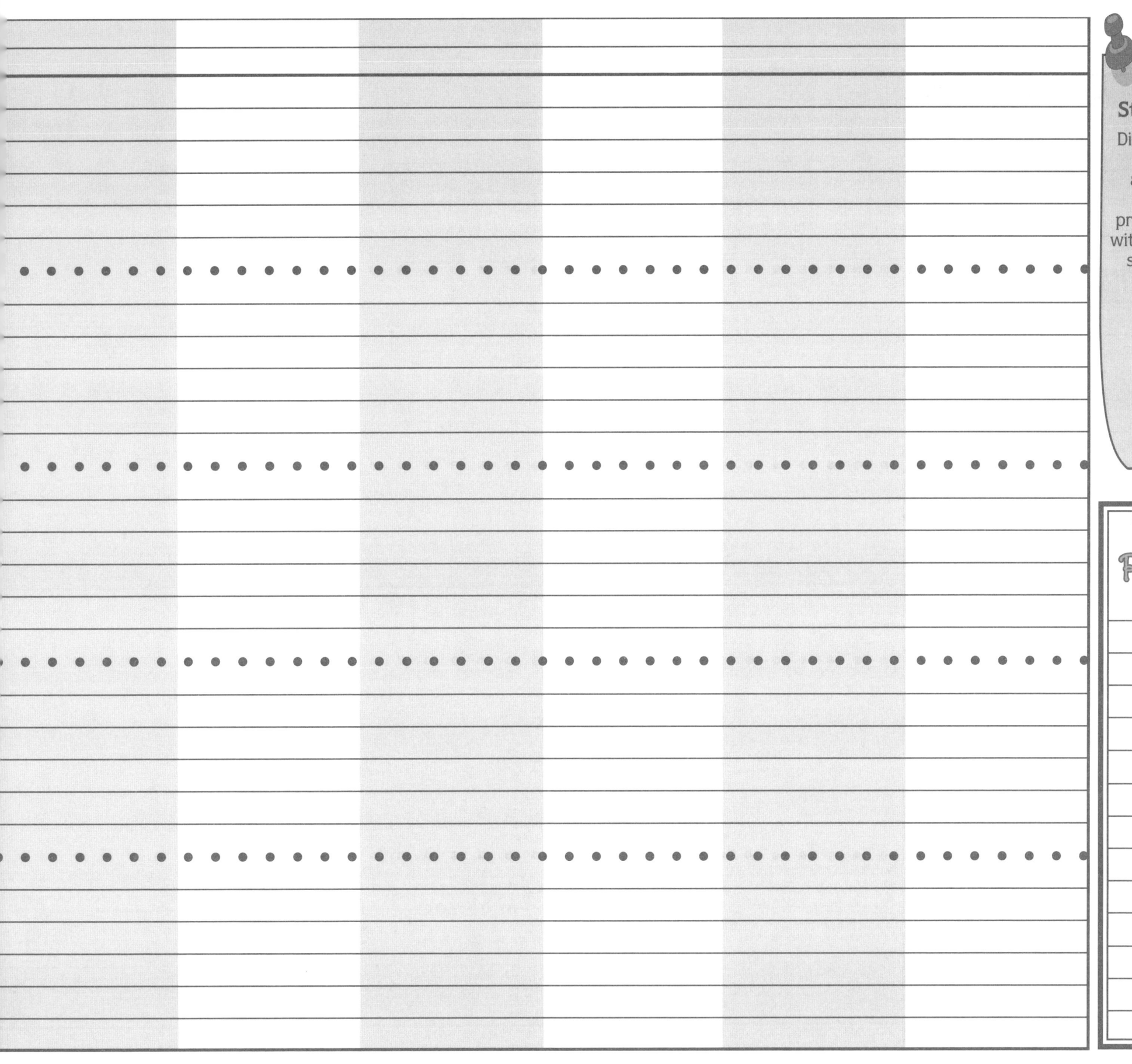

Student Work on Display

Display student work in sheet protectors for a nice look and to keep work in great condition. Attach sheet protectors to a bulletin board with thumbtacks. Then, simply slide student work into the protectors for neat and easy displays.

Things to Remember

© Carson-Dellosa • CD-104069

Week of _____	Subject _____ Time						
Monday Date: Absences:	Take Note						
Tuesday Date: Absences:	Take Note						
Wednesday Date: Absences:	Take Note						
Thursday Date: Absences:	Take Note						
Friday Date: Absences:	Take Note						

© Carson-Dellosa • CD-10406

New Student, No Problem

Welcoming a new student after the school year has begun can be quite overwhelming. Be prepared for new students and make them feel welcome. Always have several new student packets on hand. Each new student packet should include a welcome letter, required school forms for parents, a copy of your weekly classroom schedule, and any other important information. You may also want to include a small treat, such as stickers or a pencil. Having new student packets ready in advance can be a time-saver.

Things to Remember

Week of _____	Subject _____ Time					
Monday Date: Absences:	Take Note					
Tuesday Date: Absences:	Take Note					
Wednesday Date: Absences:	Take Note					
Thursday Date: Absences:	Take Note					
Friday Date: Absences:	Take Note					

© Carson-Dellosa • CD-104069

Project Teamwork

Class assignments can be much more interesting and fun when they are completed with partners or teams. When students work together as a team, it can foster creativity. Varied learning levels, talents, interests, and prior knowledge merge to enhance the amount of information learned and retained. Above all, there is an increase in the level of communication skills, and assignments become fun projects.

Things to Remember

Week of _____	Subject _____ Time					
Monday Date: Absences:	Take Note					
Tuesday Date: Absences:	Take Note					
Wednesday Date: Absences:	Take Note					
Thursday Date: Absences:	Take Note					
Friday Date: Absences:	Take Note					

Testing

Have students use file folders to cover their papers during testing. Allow students to personalize their folders by decorating them with craft materials. This is a simple, affordable tool that can also serve as an art project!

Things to Remember

© Carson-Dellosa • CD-104069

Curriculum Web Sites

The Complete Plan Book

Curriculum resources are very helpful when planning lessons; learning new, valuable teaching tools; and staying current and up-to-date with the latest national and state learning standards. The following are just some of the valuable Web sites that abound on the information superhighway.

United States Department of Education
http://www.ed.gov

National Education Association
http://www.nea.org

Council of Ministers of Education, Canada
http://www.cmec.ca/educmin.en.stm

Education News
http://www.educationnews.org

Education Week
http://www.edweek.org

Association for Supervision and Curriculum Development
http://www.ascd.org

National Council of Teachers of Mathematics
http://www.nctm.org

International Reading Association
http://www.reading.org

National Science Teachers Association
http://www.nsta.org

National Council for the Social Studies
http://www.socialstudies.org

Alabama Department of Education
http://www.alsde.edu

Alaska Department of Education & Early Development
http://www.educ.state.ak.us

Arizona Department of Education
http://www.ade.state.az.us

Arkansas Department of Education
http://arkedu.state.ar.us

California Department of Education
http://goldmine.cde.ca.gov

Colorado Department of Education
http://cde.state.co.us

Connecticut State Department of Education
http://www.state.ct.us/sde

Delaware Department of Education
http://www.doe.state.de.us

District of Columbia Public Schools
http://www.k12.dc.us

Florida Department of Education
http://www.firn.edu/doe

Georgia Department of Education
http://www.doe.k12.ga.us

Hawaii Department of Education
http://doe.k12.hi.us

Idaho Department of Education
http://www.sde.state.id.us

Illinois State Board of Education
http://www.isbe.state.il.us

Indiana Department of Education
http://doe.state.in.us

Iowa Department of Education
http://www.state.ia.us/educate

Kansas State Department of Education
http://www.ksbe.state.ks.us

Kentucky Department of Education
http://www.kde.state.ky.us

Louisiana Department of Education
http://www.doe.state.la.us

Maine State Department of Education
http://www.state.me.us/education

Maryland State Department of Education
http://marylandpublicschools.org

Massachusetts Department of Education
http://www.doe.mass.edu

Michigan Department of Education
http://michigan.gov/mde

Minnesota Department of Education
http://education.state.mn.us

Mississippi Department of Education
http://www.mde.k12.ms.us

Missouri Department of Elementary and Secondary Education
http://www.dese.state.mo.us

Montana Office of Public Instruction
http://www.opi.state.mt.us

Nebraska Department of Education
http://www.nde.state.ne.us

Nevada Department of Education
http://www.nde.state.nv.us

New Hampshire Department of Education
http://www.ed.state.nh.us

New Jersey Department of Education
http://www.state.nj.us/education

New Mexico Public Education Department
http://www.sde.state.nm.us

New York State Education Department
http://www.nysed.gov

North Carolina Department of Public Instruction
http://www.ncpublicschools.org

North Dakota Department of Public Instruction
http://www.dpi.state.nd.us

Ohio Department of Education
http://www.ode.state.oh.us

Oklahoma State Department of Education
http://www.sde.state.ok.us

Oregon Department of Education
http://www.ode.state.or.us

Pennsylvania Department of Education
http://www.pde.state.pa.us

Rhode Island Department of Elementary and Secondary Education
http://www.ridoe.net

South Carolina Department of Education
http://www.myscschools.com

South Dakota Department of Education
http://www.state.sd.us/deca

Tennessee Department of Education
http://www.state.tn.us/education

Texas Education Agency
http://www.tea.state.tx.us

Utah State Office of Education
http://www.usoe.k12.ut.us

Vermont Department of Education
http://www.state.vt.us/educ

Virginia Department of Education
http://www.pen.k12.va.us

Washington Office of Superintendent of Public Instruction
http://www.k12.wa.us

West Virginia Department of Education
http://wvde.state.wv.us

Wisconsin Department of Public Instruction
http://www.dpi.state.wi.us

Wyoming Department of Education
http://www.k12.wy.us/index.asp